105040314

P9-CRZ-936

THE STRUGGLE INTO THE 1990's

A HISTORY OF BLACK PEOPLE FROM 1968 TO THE PRESENT

Written by:
Stuart Kallen

McLean County Unit #5
Carlock IMC - 105

Published by Abdo & Daughters, 6535 Cecilia Circle, Edina, Minnesota 55439

Library bound edition distributed by Rockbottom Books, Pentagon Tower, P.O. Box 36036, Minneapolis, Minnesota 55435

Copyright© 1990 by Abdo Consulting Group, Inc., Pentagon Tower, P.O. Box 36036, Minneapolis, Minnesota 55435. International copyrights reserved in all countries. No part of this book may be reproduced in any form without written permission from the publisher. Printed in the United States.

Library of Congress Number: 90-083620   ISBN: 1-56239-021-X

Cover Illustrations by: Marlene Kallen
Inside Photos by: Wide World Photos and UPI/Bettmann Newsphotos

Cover Illustrations by: Marlene Kallen

Edited by: Rosemary Wallner

TABLE OF CONTENTS

CHAPTER 1
THE SEVENTIES

As the 1970's began, it seemed that black people were riding full speed ahead on the road to equality in the United States. Thurgood Marshall, a black lawyer, was appointed to the United States Supreme Court in 1967. Carl Stokes was elected mayor of Cleveland, Ohio, the same year, making him the first black mayor of a large Northern city. In the South, voters elected black people as mayors, councilpeople, and sheriffs. These elections took place in cities where blacks had been beaten, harassed, and killed for demanding equality only a few years earlier.

But other factors pointed out problems that lay ahead for the black struggle. Between 1960 and 1970, over three million black people moved from rural areas to large cities. During those same years, over 2.5 million white people moved out of large cities to segregated suburbs. This so-called "white flight" from the cities resulted in fewer businesses, fewer jobs, and less money for the growing black population.

Years of Violence

The late sixties and early seventies were marred by violence in many cities. After the death of Martin Luther King, Jr., in 1968, major riots erupted in dozens of cities. Hundreds of people were killed and wounded. Fires and looting caused property damage totaling hundreds of millions of dollars. Some people felt that the nonviolent methods of the early Civil Rights Movement were not effective in ending discrimination. Anger built to a flash point as cities went up in flames.

On May 14, 1970, two black students were killed and twelve were wounded at a demonstration at Jackson State College in Mississippi. The students were protesting President Richard Nixon's invasion of Cambodia. The invasion was an expansion of the Vietnam War in which many young men were dying. Many black people felt that they should not be fighting in Vietnam while being denied equal rights in the United States. The demonstration at Jackson State was also a protest against the killing of four white students at Kent State University ten days earlier. The Kent State killings of white students received national attention from the American public. The Jackson State killings of blacks went largely unnoticed.

A Prison Riot

On September 9, 1971, hundreds of black inmates took over the state prison in Attica, New York. The prisoners demanded better living conditions, food, and schooling. For four days, the prisoners held several guards as hostages. Tensions mounted as food supplies ran low. Hundreds of New York State troopers surrounded the prison and police helicopters circled overhead.

Specialists talked to the prisoners and listened to their demands. After the negotiators agreed to help the prisoners, they left the prison. Then Governor Nelson Rockefeller ordered the police to attack. Fifteen hundred New York State troopers stormed the prison and opened fire on the inmates. The police killed thirty-two inmates. The police also killed ten guards who had been hostages. An investigation showed that many of the prisoners were shot while trying to surrender. After the uprising, conditions at the prison got even worse.

Inmates at the state prison in Attica, New York, are shown here with their hands raised behind their heads. Ten guards and thirty-two inmates were killed before order was restored at the maximum security facility.

Busing

The government had ordered schools to integrate in 1955. But by 1970 hundreds of schools in the United States were all black. In many of these schools, basic items such as paper and pencils were in short supply. The schools for black students were usually old, decaying buildings in inner-city neighborhoods. While white schools had money for sports teams and proms, most inner-city schools could not even afford books. Once again, black parents who wanted better education for their children looked to the courts to remedy this situation.

In 1971, the Supreme Court ordered schools to use school buses to achieve integration. White students were bused to black schools and black students were bused to white schools. Like every other decision to integrate, this one met with great resistance. In 1972, President Nixon asked Congress to pass a law prohibiting busing. Congress refused. Busing became federal policy despite Nixon's objections.

Busing in Boston

In 1974, Federal Judge Arthur Garrity ruled that the city of Boston, Massachusetts, must bus 17,000 students to achieve racial equality.

Garrity said that Boston's black schools were "the most crowded, the oldest, the least maintained, and the most poorly staffed."

When school started at South Boston High in September 1974, 90 percent of the white students stayed home. Black students who were bused in from the Roxbury ghetto were pelted with stones. When the students left school, they were showered with shattered glass as rocks crashed through bus windows. For weeks, white parents surrounded Boston's high schools screaming racial insults at the black students. Inside the schools, fifteen to twenty fights a day took place between black and white students.

In mid-October, a white student was stabbed by a black student at Boston's Hyde Park High School. Over 450 National Guardsmen were called out to stop the riot that followed. In December, a white mob trapped 135 black students inside South Boston High. Thousands of white adults surrounded the school. The mob threatened the lives of the black students inside for four hours. School buses parked at the school's front door to fool the mob. While the mob showered the volunteer bus drivers with stones, the black students snuck out the school's back door.

Motorcycle police escort school buses as they leave South Boston High School. Some buses were stoned and several arrests were made.

School officials ordered an early Christmas vacation that streched to a month. When thirty-one black students returned to school in January, they were guarded by 500 police officers.

By 1976, over 20,000 white students had fled Boston's public schools. Most of them went to private schools or moved from the city. Soon, only black students were left in the publc schools. Because of this, Boston's schools were once again segregated.

Affirmative Action

Affirmative action is another method the United States government uses to achieve racial balance. Affirmative action programs are set up by large companies to hire blacks, women, and other minorities for jobs that would normally go to white males. President John F. Kennedy first coined the phrase "affirmative action" in 1961. Kennedy wanted black people hired by companies that had contracts with the government. In 1965, President Lyndon Johnson set specific percentages of black people that companies must hire. The percentage of blacks at a company had to be the same percentage of blacks in the surrounding community.

In other words, if a company was in a neighborhood that was 20 percent black, then the company had to find, hire, and promote blacks until the company had 20 percent black workers. The Supreme Court supported affirmative action and fined large companies that did not follow the hiring guidelines. Affirmative action was also used in colleges and universities.

Like busing, many white people were against affirmative action. Businesses were not accustomed to the government intruding in their affairs. They resented the government telling them who to hire and who to promote. White students who could not get into certain colleges felt "reverse discrimination." They said that black students had an unfair advantage because the government set aside openings in schools for them. Some white workers also felt that unqualified blacks were promoted only because of their skin color. Many black people argued that education and jobs could help reverse 350 years of slavery and discrimination.

In 1978, Allan Bakke, a white Vietnam veteran, was turned down by a dozen medical schools. One of the schools, the University of California at Davis, had a policy of affirmative action. Sixteen of the one hundred openings in the medical school were automatically reserved for blacks, Hispanics, and other minorities. Many of these students had grade averages and test scores well below those of Bakke.

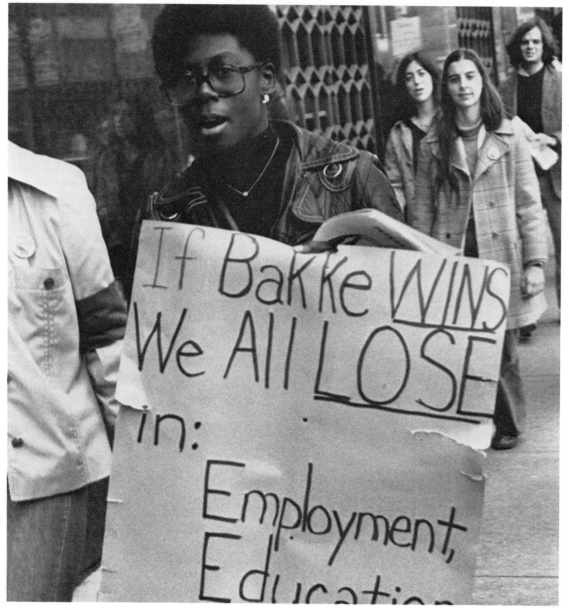

A group of about 100 protesters picketed Allan Bakke's claim that he was discriminated against.

For four years, Bakke fought affirmative action in the courts. As the case wound its way through the courts, hundreds of questions surfaced. How should the government help people who it had shut out for hundreds of years? At what cost? The Civil Rights Act of 1965 guaranteed equal rights to all people. Does it apply to white people who can't attend college or find a job because of racial quotas? Do white people have an automatic advantage because of better schools and more opportunities? The case became a judge's nightmare. Hundreds of organizations fought the issue on one side or another. The court ruled to admit Bakke to Davis. It left intact some forms of affirmative action but weakened the policy. Soon, hundreds of white people began to challenge affirmative action in the courts. Little by little, the policy was chipped away.

An example of how affirmative action helps blacks can be demonstrated by considering the shortage of doctors in poor neighborhoods. Many poor, inner-city neighborhoods have only one or two doctors. Most of these doctors are from minorities. They were students who were able to attend college because of affirmative action. If affirmative action programs were discontinued, many of these neighborhoods would have fewer doctors and other professionals.

Affirmative Action Today

In the summer of 1989, the Supreme Court heard three cases about affirmative action. In all three cases, the Supreme Court ruled against blacks, women, and minorities. In one case, white firefighters in Birmingham, Alabama, claimed they were victims of reverse discrimination because blacks were promoted in greater numbers. The Supreme Court agreed. Once the court ruled in favor of the whites, employers all over the country decided to abandon affirmative action hiring practices. Supreme Court rulings decide the way that courts all over the country decide what the law means. In this and the other rulings, the court reversed twenty years of equal opportunity hiring practices. Many minorities are hoping that the United States Congress will pass a new Civil Rights Act setting new affirmative action goals.

Advancement in the Seventies

The protests, marches, sit-ins, and demonstrations of the 1960's began to pay off for black people in the 1970's. From the city council chambers to the national political arena, voters elected black people to public office in greater numbers than ever before.

In 1972, Shirley Chisholm became the first black women to run for the office of president of the United States. She lost the nomination to George McGovern. The elections of 1972 saw Georgia's Andrew Young elected to Congress. Young was the first black congressman from the deep South in seventy years. Also elected for the first time in 1972 were Barbara Jordan (Texas), Yvonne Burke (California), and Senator Edward Brooke (Massachusetts). Alabama elected two black mayors. Thomas Bradley was elected mayor of Los Angeles. Maynard Jackson was elected mayor of Atlanta. Coleman Young was elected mayor of Detroit, Michigan.

In 1976, Georgia's Governor Jimmy Carter was elected president of the United States. When he was governor, Carter was popular with blacks because he appointed many black advisors. As president, Carter appointed Patricia Harris as Secretary of Housing and Urban Development (HUD), making her the first black woman to be a Cabinet officer. Carter appointed Andrew Young, the black mayor of Atlanta, as the American

Ambassador to the United Nations. Young spoke out against racism in Africa and other parts of the world.

President Jimmy Carter, Corretta King, Martin Luther King's widow, and Andrew Young.

The Freedom of Information Act

Another law that helped black people in the seventies was the Freedom of Information Act (FOIA). The law allowed secret documents from the Federal Bureau of Investigation (FBI) and other government agencies to be released for public scrutiny. The government released hundreds of documents detailing the extent of FBI harassment of black organizations in the sixties. For years, the FBI sought to discredit Martin Luther King, Jr. and his organization, the Southern Christian Leadership Convention (SCLC). The FBI also waged a campaign to disrupt, discredit, and "neutralize" other black groups like the Black Panthers and Black Muslims. This information led to stricter controls of the FBI's domestic spy programs. These controls were reversed during the Reagan Administration in the 1980's.

CHAPTER 2
THE EIGHTIES

As the 1980's dawned, black people faced new and complex problems in an ever changing world. The economy in the United States was slowing down. This caused a huge rise in unemployment. Inflation caused the price of almost everything to rise. The government spent billions of dollars more than it was taking in. Government programs that helped black people started meeting resistance by white voters and politicians. As more white people competed for fewer jobs, programs like affirmative action came under attack.

During the sixties, the black struggle was one of the main focuses of the national news media. During the eighties, Hispanics, women, the disabled, the elderly, and even white males adopted the language of the black equal rights movement. With so many groups demanding "equal rights," the black struggle received less attention. There was less money for the equality struggle and more people competing for it.

Reaganomics

Republican Ronald Reagan was elected president on November 4, 1980. Reagan did not believe that the government could solve black people's problems. In his inaugural address, he said, "Government is the problem not the solution." Reagan decided to reverse the whole range of federal programs that had been in place for almost fifty years.

Reagan cut taxes and spending on social programs. The Congressional Quarterly from 1981 shows that Reagan cut 24 *billion* dollars from social services. The number of people living in poverty swelled from 29 million to 35 million. The number of people living in poverty included one out of every seven Americans. The budget ax fell on black and white alike.

President Ronald Reagan (left), talks to the media after meeting with Jesse Jackson about Operation PUSH (People United to Serve Humanity).

According to the New York *Times*, the gulf between rich and the poor became wider than ever. People in the inner-cities were least able to afford cutbacks in employment-training programs and unemployment benefits. The New York *Times* states that by 1984, one out of every three black people lived in poverty.

The Reagan administration also wanted to cut other departments. The New York *Times* stated in 1985 that the Department of Justice cut the number of lawyers defending civil rights from 210 to 52.

On September 19, 1981, over 300,000 people demonstrated in Washington, D.C. They protested Reagan's policies. On August 28, 1983, over 250,000 people marched on Washington and called for jobs and equal opportunities.

Gains in the Eighties

In spite of the federal government's inaction on civil rights, there were many gains for blacks in the eighties. As in other years, the Ku Klux Klan and other racist groups organized racial beatings, bombings, and armed robberies to finance their organizations. But the FBI had many spies within the Ku Klux Klan. In 1987, members of the Florida Realm of the United Klans of America were indicted for trying to overthrow the government. They were given long prison sentences.

In Mobile, Alabama, in 1981, a black teenager was murdered by Klansmen and left hanging from a tree. The teenager's family sued the Klan for 7 million dollars and won. The Klan had to sell its national headquarters in Tuscaloosa, Alabama, to pay the lawsuit. Because of legal and financial difficulties, Klan membership dropped from 10,000 in 1981 to less than 5,500 by 1987.

Black voting rights have been the greatest
success of the Civil Rights Movement. Since the
Voting Rights Act of 1965, the number of
registered black voters has doubled. In 1965, less
than 100 blacks held elective offices. In 1989, that
number was over 6,800. That includes twenty-four
congressmen and three hundred mayors. The
most dramatic change was in Mississippi. In the
late 1980's, that state led the nation in the number
of black officials (578). In 1989, David Dinkins
became the first black mayor of New York City.
That same year in Virginia, Douglas Wilder
became the first black governor in the United
States history.

The days of fighting for integrated schools in the
South seemed like ancient history by the end of
the eighties. All across the South, black and white
children began to attend the same schools. There
are still all-white private schools, but in general,
segregated schools are a thing of the past.

Douglas Wilder, the first black governor elected in the United States.

David Dinkins, the first black mayor of New York City.

In the field of entertainment superstars like Eddie Murphy, Whitney Houston, Arsenio Hall, Oprah Winfrey, Tracey Chapman, Michael Jackson, L.L. Kool J, Bill Cosby, Spike Lee, and hundreds of others, set the styles in music, movies, and fashion for the entire world.

In the business world, over 200,000 black men and women became corporate managers in the eighties. Although blacks found it difficult to rise to the top in many companies, major corporations could no longer ignore the talent and drive of black executives.

George Bush

George Walker Bush was elected president of the United States in November 1988. In his first months in office, Bush named Dr. Louis Sullivan as the Secretary of Health and Human Services. The only black person to head a department in Bush's Cabinet, Sullivan promised to improve health care for millions of America's poor. Sullivan spoke out against cigarette and liquor advertising targeted at black consumers. Bush also named several blacks as ambassadors and to important departments in his Cabinet. President Bush's wife, Barbara, hired Anna Perez to be her press secretary. Perez is the first black woman to act as press secretary for a first lady. Many black people are hoping to make new gains under the Bush administration.

President Bush gives a speech on the prevalence of Drugs in our society.

CHAPTER 3
THE STRUGGLE INTO THE NINETIES

As the twentieth century draws to a close, new and complicated problems face black people. One of the biggest problems is drugs.

When the earning power of blacks and whites fell sharply in the eighties, some of them turned to drug dealing. When unemployment among youths rose to over 40 percent, many drug dealers recruited this pool of unemployed youths. Cheap cocaine flooded into America's cities as thousands of people became instant addicts of "crack."

Many American inner-cities fell into ruin as money for education, housing, job training, and city services was massively cut by the federal government. Many poor people became desperate and hopeless about the future. Drug violence increased at a record rate. In more than a dozen major cities, rival gangs of automatic weapon-toting, drug-dealing teenagers wage a bloody guerilla war for control of the thriving drug trade. Inner-city hospitals are going bankrupt as thousands of young gunshot victims fill emergency rooms. The Drug Enforcement Agency (DEA) estimated that 4,000 deaths were caused by drug-related gang violence in 1989.

President Bush's answer to the drug problem has been the "War on Drugs." Night after night, police officers raid crack houses and make gang sweeps in large cities. Night after night, hundreds of arrests are made, but the drug problem continues. Some black people complain that the drug war is racist and focused mainly on blacks. About one third of the black men in large cities are arrested on drug charges by the time they reach the age of thirty. Almost one in four black males between the ages of twenty and thirty is in prison, on probation or parole, or awaiting trial. The prisons of the United States are overcrowded to the point of breaking. And the drug violence continues.

Some Solutions

In housing projects in Chicago, blacks and whites organized committees to kick drug dealers out of their apartments. In other cities, community leaders rallied in front of drug houses with bullhorns and picket signs scaring the dealers out of the neighborhood. In Washington, D.C., Black Muslims organized patrols to get rid of drug dealers. In cities all across the country, people are taking control of their neighborhoods. Black people who fought for freedom from racism in the sixties are now fighting for freedom from drug slavery in the nineties.

Many people feel that education and treatment are the best way out of the drug crises. Kurt Shmoke, the black mayor of Baltimore in the early nineties, thought that if the government spent as much money on treatment and education as it did on prisons, the drug crises could be solved in a few years. Shmoke said, "We need to educate and offer meaningful employment opportunities to the millions of young Americans who are using drugs out of despair and selling drugs as a means of economic survival."

CHAPTER 4
BLACK LEADERS OF TODAY

Jesse Jackson — 1941-
Civil Rights Leader

If anybody could be said to be carrying on the work of Dr. Martin Luther King, Jr., it is Jesse Jackson. From the Middle East to Washington, D.C., Jesse Jackson preaches a message of equality and justice for all.

Jesse Jackson was born in Greenville, South Carolina, in 1941. He received a football scholarship to the University of Illinois after he graduated from Sterling High School. After a short while, Jackson transferred to North Carolina Agricultural and Technical College in Greensboro. While there, Jackson became involved in the sit-ins that were helping desegregate the South.

Jackson continued to be involved in the civil rights movement while he attended Chicago Theological Seminary. While Jackson was protesting segregation in Selma, Alabama, in 1965, he met Dr. Martin Luther King, Jr. Soon, Jackson became a member of King's staff.

Jesse Jackson (left), stands on a balcony with Dr. Martin Luther King, Jr. (middle). This photograph was taken on April 3, 1968, the day before an assassins bullet killed Martin Luther King.

33

Jackson then returned to Chicago to head King's "Campaign to End Slums."

In 1965, Jackson also became the head of King's "Operation Breadbasket" in Chicago. Operation Breadbasket's purpose was to help expand job opportunities for blacks. Under Jackson's direction, Operation Breadbasket became very successful. Jackson organized boycotts of businesses that discriminated against black people. Because of Operation Breadbasket, many companies started hiring blacks, using black-owned banks, and contracting with black-owned service companies.

In 1971, Jackson founded operation PUSH (People United to Serve Humanity). PUSH threatened to boycott large companies such as Coca-Cola and Burger King unless they set up black distributors, advertised in black newspapers, and hired black workers. The operation was a success. PUSH branches were set up in several cities. In 1976, Jackson began PUSH for Excellence. This program helped black students attend college.

Jackson became involved in politics when he realized that the best way for black people to have more power was to elect black mayors, governors, senators, congressmen, and others.

Jackson toured the country helping blacks register to vote.

Jackson soon became interested in world affairs. In 1979, he went to the Middle East to try to end the struggles between Israel, Lebanon, Syria, Egypt, and Palestine. While in the Middle East, Jackson met with the leaders of those countries. Unfortunately, his peace talks did little to solve the problems in that part of the world.

In 1984, Robert Goodman, a black U.S. Navy pilot, was shot down over Lebanon. Jackson used his friendship with Syrian leader Hafiz al-Assad to obtain the release of Goodman. Later that year, Jackson traveled to Cuba and helped free twenty-two Americans and twenty-six Cubans who were held in prison there.

Besides his globe-spanning missions in 1984, Jackson also ran for president of the United States. Jackson wasn't the first black person to run for president. But Jackson gained major support, receiving as much as 87 percent of the black vote. To gain white voter support, Jackson put together the "Rainbow Coalition." The coalition addressed the needs of women, the poor, Hispanics, and other voters who felt that the government was ignoring their needs.

Jesse Jackson (left) meets with Palestine Liberation Organization Chief Yasir Arafat in Beirut in 1979.

Jackson did not get the Democratic nomination. But he proved that a black candidate could get major voter support.

In 1988, Jackson ran for president again. Like before, he did not receive the Democratic nomination, but he broadened his power base even further.

From the sit-ins in the South to national presidential politics, Jesse Jackson proved that black people are ready to lead America. His slogan, "I am somebody!" is echoed by young people across the country. Jesse Jackson keeps the dream alive.

Guion Stewart Bluford, Jr. — 1942-
Astronaut

"Five, four, three, two, one, lift-off!" The space shuttle *Challenger* lit up the early morning sky on August 30, 1983. Inside, Guion Bluford, Jr., made history as the first black astronaut.

Guion Bluford was born in 1942 in Philadelphia, Pennsylvania. After joining the Air Force in 1964, Bluford flew 144 combat missions during the Vietnam War. Bluford was given over twenty-four medals and awards for his skill and bravery in the Air Force. After his duty in Vietnam, Bluford enrolled in the Air Force Institute of Technology where he studied aerospace engineering. After several years of study, Bluford received a Ph.D. degree.

In 1978, Bluford was accepted in the astronaut training program at the National Aeronautics and Space Administration (NASA). Bluford learned astronomy, geology, medicine, and communications at Johnson Space Flight Center in Houston, Texas. He also learned to work with the computer, power systems, and instruments that controlled the space shuttle.

Guion Bluford, Jr., America's first black astronaut.

In August 1983, Bluford began a six-day flight, circling 180 miles above the earth in the *Challenger*. During the flight, Bluford did medical tests and launched a communications and weather satellite. On September 5, Bluford and the *Challenger* crew landed at Edwards Air Force Base in California.

In October 1985, Bluford was a crew member on another *Challenger* mission. By the end of this mission, Bluford had spent over thirteen days in space. Bluford paved the way for other black astronauts such as Colonel Fred Gregory and Major Charlie Bolden. A black woman astronaut, Dr. Mae Jemison is in training for a space mission. Dr. Ronald McNair died in the *Challenger* explosion in 1986.

By serving his country in war and improving his education during peace, Guion Bluford proved that a black person can fly high for the United States.

CHAPTER 5
NELSON MANDELA

Although Nelson Mandela is not an American, his cause has been adopted by American blacks and people of all colors all over the world. Mandela's homeland, South Africa, is one of the last countries on earth were blatant discrimination is written into the law. In the 1990's, when Mandela speaks for freedom in South Africa, he speaks for freedom fighters everywhere.

When Nelson Mandela was a young boy, he loved to sit around the fire and listen to the stories of the tribal elders. As the fire burned into the night, the elders would talk about the life in Africa before the arrival of the white men from Europe. "Our people lived peacefully, under the democratic rule of the kings," Mandela later recalled. "We moved freely up and down the country without hinderance. The country was ours . . . we occupied the land, the forests, the rivers; we extracted the mineral wealth beneath the soil and all the riches of this beautiful country. We set up and operated our own government, we controlled our own armies, and we organized our own trade and commerce."

By the time Mandela was born on July 18, 1918, those days were just a memory. Mandela grew up in a world where white Europeans ruled his country. But those stories of the old days inspired him to devote his life to regaining the rights of his people. His tribal name, *Rolihlahla*, pointed the way of Nelson's future. His name means "stirring up trouble."

Mandela's father was a respected tribal chief. He taught young Nelson about the British and Dutch settlers who came to South Africa with guns. The Europeans shot the blacks who were armed only with spears. They forced the blacks to be slaves and also brought people from India to work as slaves. In 1910, despite protests from Africans, the British government gave one million white South Africans, known as *Afrikaners*, control over 4.5 million "nonwhites." The Afrikaners passed laws to restrict the movements of the blacks. They could not move freely in their own country and were forced to live in "reserves." The laws were enforced with clubs and guns. When Mandela was young, he heard the history of "rivers running red with African blood."

In 1930, when Mandela was twelve years old, his father died. Nelson went to a Methodist boarding school where he practiced traditional tribal customs while getting a Bachelor of Arts degree. Mandela's studies were cut short when he was suspended for taking place in a student strike.

Life in Johannesburg

When Mandela was twenty-two years old, he moved to the noisy, fast-paced city of Johannesburg. The train he had ridden on was marked by a sign that said "for Non-Europeans." In Johannesburg, Mandela found that the buses, restaurants, cafes, and public restrooms were labeled "Europeans Only." Even the park benches carried this label. Mandela did not see much of the white part of town. Soon he was in one of the "native" locations.

In the black section of town, there was no electricity, telephones, sewers, plumbing, or tarred roads. The police constantly raided the area, looking for blacks without "passes." Like all blacks in the city, Mandela now needed a pass to get a job, live in a town, travel, and be out after the eleven o'clock curfew. Without a pass, he would be imprisoned.

Nelson Mandela in his law office in Johannesburg, South Africa in 1952.

Mandela was lucky to find work as a lawyer in an all-white firm. He married his first wife, Ntoko Mase and moved to a section of Johannesburg known as Soweto. Mandela got involved with the African National Congress (ANC) while living in Soweto. The ANC was founded in 1912 by four African lawyers who were trained in Britain and the United States. The ANC wanted to unite the African people against the European repression.

The Laws of Apartheid

In 1948, the Afrikaner National Party came to power in South Africa and passed a series of laws known as *apartheid*. The policy of apartheid classified each person according to race or tribe. There were dozens of classifications from "Asian-African" to "Indian-Bantu." The towns and rural areas of South Africa were divided into zones in which only one race could live, own property, and conduct business. All the best areas were set aside for white people.

The government closed all schools and universities to nonwhites. It then set up schools for nonwhites that taught such activities as "tree planting" and "sheep herding."

Apartheid created laws that segregated every aspect of South African life. It created *townships* where nonwhites had to live. The townships were outside big cities where cheap labor was needed. Women now had to carry passes. Blacks not needed for labor were sent to *homelands*. Although blacks made up 70 percent of the people in South Africa, the homelands occupied only thirteen percent of the land. Usually a man working in the city could not have his wife and children live with him in the township. They had to live hundreds of miles away in the homeland. Because of this, families were separated most of the year.

All forms of protest against apartheid were stopped by a law called the Suppression of Communism Act of 1951. Using the Communist threat as an excuse, the law made it illegal to oppose the government. Books were banned, newspapers were censored, free speech was stopped, and political meetings were outlaws.

Mandela Reacts

Naturally, Mandela and the ANC were alarmed with the apartheid laws. In 1949, Mandela organized thousands of people to peacefully resist apartheid. Mandela toured the country addressing meetings and organizing people. The laws made travel difficult, and sometimes Mandela had to walk miles and sleep under the nearest tree.

Apartheid protests began all over South Africa. Some blacks marched into "European Only" areas. Some refused to carry passes. Over 8,500 blacks were arrested. The government reacted by making stricter laws. The membership of the ANC climbed from 7,000 to 100,000 people. Mandela was put on trial and sentenced to nine months in prison. The government then passed a law against political leaders like Mandela.

Although Mandela did not want to be a leader, he was elected president of the Johannesburg ANC. His personal magnetism and electrifying speeches made him a born leader. Before he could take over leadership, he was *banned* by the government. Banning was the main weapon that the government used to silence leaders like Mandela and hundreds of others. Because he was banned, Mandela could not leave Johannesburg, attend meetings, or meet with more than one other person at a time. Mandela continued to practice law, raise his three sons, and work for the ANC in secret.

Mandela Is Arrested
BANG! BANG! "Open up. Police!" At dawn on December 5, 1956, Nelson Mandela and hundreds of others were arrested for violating the Suppression of Communism Act. Mandela knew some Communists and believed in some Communist philosophies, but he did not consider himself a Communist. Nonetheless, the government used the act to charge Mandela. When the trial started, thousands of protestors gathered around the courthouse singing freedom songs. Eventually, Mandela was released on bail.

For the next five years, Mandela had to fight for his survival in a courtroom. He worked part-time as a lawyer, but the trial put a strain on his marriage. Eventually Mandela was divorced. In 1958, he met and married Winnie Mandela. They had two daughters.

Nelson Mandela (center) looks through a newspaper with then ANC President Dr. James Moroka (left) and Indian Congress President Yusuf Dadoo.

49

In March 1960, after Mandela had been on trial for over four years, a protest was held in Sharpeville Township. The police fired into a crowd killing sixty-nine people and wounding two hundred. Many people were shot in the back, some of the victims were children. Horror and rage swept through the country. All over South Africa there were riots, strikes, and protest marches in the streets.

The South African government declared a state of emergency and banned the ANC. Mandela was imprisoned. But during his trial, Mandela had made a good impression on American and British observers. The ANC cause became known in political circles in Europe and America.

On March 29, 1961, Mandela was found guilty. He was temporarily released. When he left the courtroom, he was carried on the shoulders of a cheering, dancing crowd.

Mandela Goes Underground

After the trial, Mandela returned to his home and told Winnie, "Darling, just pack a few of my clothes in a suitcase. I'm going away for a long time." Wearing a long coat and a hat pulled down over his face, Mandela went underground. He took over leadership of the ANC and organized strikes and protests while on the run. It was hard for such a well-known man to hide, and he had some narrow escapes. One time he had to slide down a rope from a second-story apartment to escape the police who were coming up the stairs. His daring escapes made him a legend in the African community.

During his period on the run, Mandela decided that sabotage was the answer to fight apartheid. Mandela formed the Spear of the Nation and started blowing up telegraph lines. Although Mandela and the Spear of the Nation would use violence against government property, they vowed never to kill human beings. During this period, Mandela traveled to London and Algeria to speak to political leaders. He was thrilled when, in other countries, he saw blacks and whites working, shopping, and living together. When he returned to South Africa on August 5, 1962, Mandela was captured. Three cars of police officers cornered him as he drove down a road near Durban. In 1990, the United States Central Intelligence Agency (CIA) admitted that they had used their resources to help the South African government capture Mandela. He had been underground for seventeen months.

Mandela was sentenced to five years in prison. While in prison, he was put on trial for the sabotage he had done while underground. This time he was sentenced to life in prison.

Mandela was taken to Robben Island Maximum Security Prison. Robben Island Prison is on a cold, damp island near Cape Town. Mandela was given a short sleeve shirt and a pair of short pants. Those clothes gave him no protection from the bitter cold. The prison food was corn mush and coffee. The days became years as Mandela broke rocks in the prison limestone quarry. Every six months he was allowed to write and receive one letter and visit one person for thirty minutes. During this period, Mandela lost fifty pounds. When Winnie came to visit, they were only able to see each other through a small glass window. They talked through a telephone. Mandela was not allowed to write a diary or see a newspaper.

Meanwhile, Winnie was put in prison for her work with the ANC. She was tortured and spent five months in solitary confinement. After spending another ten months in jail, she was released without ever having been charged with a crime. When Winnie returned home, she was placed under house arrest — she couldn't leave her home at nights and on weekends. After two years without a visit, Winnie was finally able to see her husband — for thirty minutes.

In prison, Mandela organized hunger strikes to protest living conditions. Because of worldwide pressure on the South African government, Mandela's living conditions improved slightly. More frequent visits were allowed. Mandela was allowed to see his daughters, who were now teenagers.

Mandela was transferred to Pollsmore Prison in 1976. After ten years there the authorities tried tempting him with offers of release. "Leave the country," they said. "Stop your political organizing," they said. He turned them all down. Fearing national riots if he died in prison, the South African government moved Mandela to Victor Verster Prison Farm. There, Mandela had a swimming pool, telephone, and computers. The jailers started calling him *Mister* Mandela.

Free At Last!

On February 5, 1990, South African's President F. W. de Klerk, lifted the thirty-year ban on the ANC and said that he would release 120 political prisoners. On Sunday, February 11, Nelson Mandela walked out of prison into the waiting arms of Winnie — and the African people. Mandela had spent 10,000 days in prison — twenty-seven years. Grey-haired and thin, the seventy-one-year-old Mandela returned to Cape Town where he gave a rousing speech to tens of thousands of cheering Africans. Mandela made it clear that his age and imprisonment had not changed his goals — equal rights for South Africa's black population.

In the United States, millions of people, black and white, cheered the release of Mandela. But in South Africa, 15,000 militant whites marched through the streets chanting, "Hang Mandela!" Other black political parties disagreed with Mandela's positions and did not consider him their leader. But the first steps to a desegregated South Africa had been made. Whatever changes are in store for that country, Nelson Mandela would have a hand in making them happen.

After spending twenty-seven years in prison, Nelson Mandela was released on February 11, 1990.

Mandela in America

In June 1990, Nelson Mandela traveled to the United States. Over 750,000 people watched as Mandela rode through the streets of New York City in a huge ticker-tape parade. New York's black mayor, David Dinkins, gave Mandela the keys to the city. In speech after speech, Mandela used the words of black American heroes like Martin Luther King, Jr., Malcom X, and Marcus Garvey to call for freedom in South Africa. Black Americans cheered as Mandela screamed, "Death to racism!"

From New York, Mandela made a cross-country tour. He spoke before the Congress and Senate and received several standing ovations. Mandela spoke with President Bush and asked for America's help in the South African struggle. Mandela went to Los Angeles, Detroit, Boston, and other cities. American blacks treated Mandela like a hero everywhere he went. For American blacks, Mandela turned a spotlight on the troubles of racism. Many people felt that black problems were ignored during the 1980's. With Mandela out of prison, people once again are saying no to racism and injustice.

Nelson Mandela (center), wife Winnie, and friend sing "God Bless America."

A FINAL WORD

It has been over 370 years since the first black slave arrived in America. Slavery ended over 130 years ago. Yet black people still struggle for equality and acceptance in the 1990's. But as the century ends, black people have greater opportunities and brighter horizons than ever before. As communications and television make the world seem smaller, racism all over the globe is protested and fought. In Africa, Europe, China, and other countries, people demand equal rights and freedom using the terms and techniques that American blacks perfected during the 1960's.

There are good people and bad people of every color. In the 1990's people all over the world have learned that everyone has the same dreams and desires no matter what their skin color. The message of the nineties is that the world must unite to fight environmental problems, war, racism, and hunger. It's not "us" against "them" anymore. It's all of "us" together on one planet.

Every great black leader has said it again and again, education can solve our problems. With education and intelligence, we can "let our light shine" and make the world a better place for everyone.

Dr. Martin Luther King, Jr. in his last public appearance on April 4, 1968.

GLOSSARY

AFFIRMATIVE ACTION - An active effort to improve the employment or education of members of minority groups and women.

DESEGREGATION - The act of allowing minority groups to share facilities and activities with the majority group.

DISCRIMINATION - The unfair treatment of a minority group by the majority. Discrimination can be organized and deliberate.

INFLATION - An increase or rise in the usual or normal prices of goods and services.

INTEGRATION - The act of making something open to people of all races.

MAJORITY GROUP - The group that has the most power in a society.

MINORITY GROUP - Any group that is less powerful than the majority. Minority groups are almost always the target of discrimination.

RACIAL - Having to do with races, such as whites, blacks, Asians, and Mexicans.

RACISM - Behavior expressing dislike or hatred of another race.

SEGREGATION - The forced separation of majority and minority groups.

60

INDEX